HARD NUTS
OF HISTORY
Ancient
Rome

TRACEY TURNER
ILLUSTRATED BY JAMIE LENMAN

First published 2014 by

A & C Black, an imprint of Bloomsbury Publishing Plc

50 Bedford Square, London WC1B 3DP

www.bloomsbury.com

ISBN 978-1-4729-0561-1

A CIP catalogue for this book is available from the British Library.

Printed in China by Leo Paper Products, Heshan, Guangdong

1 3 5 7 9 10 8 6 4 2

CONTENTS

INTRODUCTION

This book contains some of the hardest nuts of ancient Rome – a selection of them, at least, because there were an awful lot of tough Romans. Some of them were brave, some were clever, some were fearsome fighters and some were absolutely awful. But all of them were as hard as nails.

FIND OUT ABOUT . . .

• Marauding barbarians

• Barrels of snakes

• A conquering warrior queen

• Poisoners, assassins, and an emperor who killed his own mother

If you've ever wanted to enter the murderous world of Roman politics, join the Roman army, or conquer Mesopotamia, read on. Follow the hard nuts to the uncivilised frontiers of the Empire, besieged cities in Gaul, and across the Alps by elephant.

As well as discovering stories of courage and cunning, you might be in for a few surprises. Did you know, for example, that Emperor Caligula's sister plotted to kill him? Or that Emperor Claudius's wife was a murderer?

You're about to meet some of the toughest people of ancient Rome . . .

Plus play the game on page 44 and see if you would have been hard enough to fight, persuade, conquer and murder your way to the top of the Roman Empire!

HANNIBAL

Hannibal was a brilliant but ruthless North African general on a mission to stop the mighty Roman Empire in its tracks.

HARD NUT RATING: 7.8

WAR WITH ROME

Hannibal was born in 247 BC in Carthage, a city-state in North Africa, the son of general Hamilcar Barca. Carthage had its own empire, which the Romans didn't like at all as they thought Rome should be the only one doing any conquering. Carthage and Rome ended up fighting one another for 20 years, in what became known as the First Punic War. In the end Carthage offered Rome the island of Sicily in exchange for peace. Rome accepted, but took Corsica and Sardinia as well – without being offered!

SPANISH CONQUESTS

Hamilcar Barca, Hannibal's father, decided to take revenge on Rome by conquering land in Spain, and took Hannibal with him. After his father died, Hannibal took over as general. By that time he was 26 and had already had some brilliant military ideas – he'd won one battle by tipping barrels of live snakes onto the deck of an enemy ship. He also planned to conquer the whole of Spain, and was making a pretty good job of it.

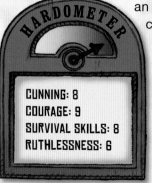

HARDOMETER

CUNNING: 8
COURAGE: 9
SURVIVAL SKILLS: 8
RUTHLESSNESS: 6

ELEPHANTS ACROSS THE ALPS

Rome was alarmed by Hannibal's progress in Spain and declared war on Carthage – again. Hannibal decided to attack Rome in a way they'd never expect:

from the north . . . with elephants! He marched 90,000 foot soldiers, 12,000 cavalry and 37 elephants from Spain, across the Pyrenees, through Gaul (now France), over the Alps and into Italy. The route – especially the mountains – was harder going than he'd thought, and the army was attacked by different tribes along the way. In the end only 26,000 men and one elephant made it into Italy. Hannibal stayed there and battled the Romans for fifteen years.

NO SURRENDER

Rome invaded Carthage and Hannibal was called back from Italy to help, but this time the Romans defeated him. Carthage agreed to peace terms. But Hannibal escaped, and carried on fighting the Romans. After many years, in about 183 BC, the Romans finally cornered Hannibal and demanded his surrender. But Hannibal chose death and killed himself by taking poison.

JOINING THE ROMAN ARMY

The Romans didn't get their Empire by asking nicely: they got it by sending in their army to kill anyone who stood in their way. Would you have been tough enough to join?

JOINING UP

You'll need to be a male Roman citizen (sorry, no girls), healthy and aged between 17 and 46, and you'll need to like marching long distances and fighting. You'll be well paid, well trained and you won't go hungry. There are a few downsides, though: you have to sign up for 25 years, agree not to marry, and be willing to fight and die for Rome.

CENTURIES, COHORTS AND LEGIONS

The ruthless Roman army was the most powerful and best organised of its time. It had a rigid structure. A lowly citizen like you would have been a foot soldier called a legionary (because you're part of a legion). Legions were organised into groups:

80 legionaries = 1 century
(a century does indeed mean a hundred: at first there were 100 legionaries in a century, but the number was reduced to 80).

6 centuries = 1 cohort

10 centuries = 1 prima cohors

9 cohorts + 1 prima cohors = 1 legion

That's 5,120 men in every legion. There were about 30 legions in the Roman army.

TOP RANKING

Everyone in the army knows his place and, as a legionary, yours is right at the bottom. A centurion is in charge of your century, and a legate is in charge of the whole legion. At the top, generals have command of several legions each. And in charge of them is the Emperor himself.

LOADING UP

Roman soldiers had to carry:

• Weapons and armour – including a metre-long javelin and a 10 kilogram shield.

• A spade for digging ditches when making camp.

• Food and cooking utensils.

• A heavy leather tent.

That's more than 30 kilograms of stuff altogether!

ROME'S LITTLE HELPERS

Not a Roman citizen? Good news! You can still become an auxiliary ('helper') soldier. Auxiliaries have fewer rights, are paid less money and given less training than legionaries, who will probably be a bit snobby about you. However, you still have to do the fighting and dying bit. But when you retire (if you live that long), you'll become a Roman citizen.

JULIUS CAESAR

Julius Caesar was a ruthless Roman leader and a brilliant general, who did lots of conquering before making himself fatally unpopular.

HARD NUT RATING: 8.3

REPUBLICAN ROME

When Julius Caesar was born, there hadn't been a king of Rome for more than 400 years. Rome was ruled by two consuls, who were elected from the Senate and ruled for a year. There were 300 senators, who looked after things like law-making and going to war, and there was also an assembly of ordinary citizens who elected the consuls. Caesar had to wait a while before he could become a senator because he was living in exile while his enemy, Sulla, was busy executing anyone he didn't like in Rome. He wisely kept his distance until Sulla died.

GOVERNING AND CONQUERING

By the time Caesar was back in Rome he had a reputation as a ruthless hard nut because of a brave brush with pirates. He landed a series of top political jobs, including governor of Spain, which gave him the chance to show off his conquering skills: he invaded Portugal, killed lots of people and brought huge amounts of loot back to Rome. He was just the kind of leader the Romans liked, and he was soon elected consul.

HARDOMETER

CUNNING: 8
COURAGE: 9
SURVIVAL SKILLS: 7
RUTHLESSNESS: 9

THREE LEADERS

Caesar decided that being consul wasn't quite powerful enough. With two hard-nut general friends, Pompey and Crassus, he took control of Rome. Then he began a conquering spree: after eight years' hard battling, Gaul (mainly what's now France and Belgium) was ruled by Rome.

ONE LEADER

Crassus was killed in battle, and Pompey and Caesar went to war over who should be in charge. Caesar came out on top. Back in Rome, Caesar was made Dictator of the Empire for a period of ten years. But this wasn't enough for power-hungry Caesar. He made himself Dictator for Life. To the Romans, this was too close to being a king. A group of 23 senators put a stop to Caesar's ambitions by stabbing him to death.

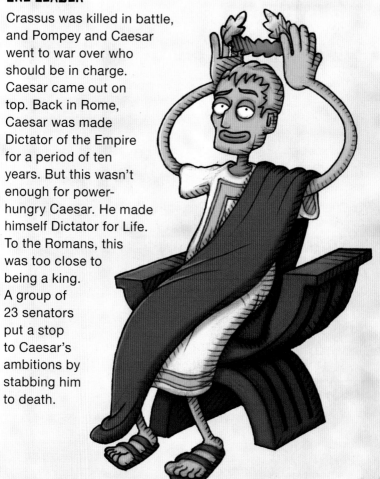

AUGUSTUS CAESAR

Augustus Caesar managed what Julius Caesar hadn't: he became the first Emperor of Rome, though he was careful not to call himself that, and ruled the entire Roman world.

HARD NUT RATING: 9

DEFEATING ENEMIES

Augustus was originally known as Octavian. He was born in Rome in 63 BC, the great-nephew of Julius Caesar, who was assassinated when Octavian was 18. Julius Caesar had named Octavian as his heir, and Octavian acted fast. In true hard-nut style, Octavian raised an army and defeated Caesar's murderers, who were led by Brutus and Cassius. His friend Mark Antony had helped Octavian defeat his enemies, and at first they agreed to share power, together with another Roman leader, Lepidus. But it wasn't long before they fell out. Octavian defeated Mark Antony at the Battle of Actium. Rome was now in his sole control.

DEFINITELY NOT A KING

Even though Octavian had all the power, he was careful not to say so and look too much like a king, which had been Julius Caesar's big mistake. Octavian called himself 'First Citizen', changed his name to Augustus, and reorganised the Roman army to make it more permanent, which helped him stay in charge and also meant he could use the army to conquer more land.

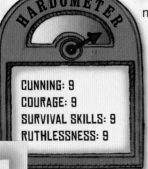

HARDOMETER

CUNNING: 9
COURAGE: 9
SURVIVAL SKILLS: 9
RUTHLESSNESS: 9

EXPANDING TERRITORIES

Augustus wanted the Empire to be a lot bigger. Under his control, the Roman army conquered Egypt, the bits of Spain that weren't already conquered, and chunks of central Europe. The barbarian tribes in Germany proved too fierce even for the Romans. Thousands of men were lost and Germany managed to stay out of the Roman Empire.

AN IMPRESSIVE EMPIRE

By the time he died in AD 14, Augustus had turned Rome from a republic, ruled by elected politicians, into an empire, ruled by an emperor who inherited his title. Rome was now much bigger (and richer), lots of impressive new buildings were built, and the Roman army was stronger. Augustus had paved the way for a long line of Roman emperors, and an empire that would last (the eastern part, at least) for nearly 1,500 years.

FIRST CITIZEN

BOUDICA

Boudica was a warrior queen in Roman Britain. She wasn't afraid to lead her tribe against the might of the Roman army.

HARD NUT RATING: 7.5

RAMPAGING ROMANS

Boudica's husband, King Prasutagas of the Iceni tribe, died in about AD 60. The Romans thought that this was their opportunity to get their hands on the land in eastern England that belonged to the Iceni. They flogged Boudica, attacked her daughters, and stole property from the Iceni tribespeople. But they had picked on the wrong woman.

REVOLTING BRITISH

Boudica raised an army of Iceni and other tribes, and led them in a revolt against the Romans. She knew that the Roman army was in charge of most of Britain, well-trained, armed to the teeth, and almost unstoppable. But she didn't care. She headed for the nearby Roman fort at Colchester, armed with war chariots, swords, and a burning sense of injustice.

AVENGING ARMY

HARDOMETER

CUNNING: 7
COURAGE: 9
SURVIVAL SKILLS: 7
RUTHLESSNESS: 7

Boudica and her army battered the Roman troops sent to fight them in Colchester. Then they turned towards London, which at the time was a fairly small trading settlement. Suetonius, the Roman governor, was busy in Wales when he got news of Boudica's revolt, and marched to London straight away.

But when he got there, he took one look at Boudica's angry army and decided to evacuate London instead of fighting.

BATTLING THE ROMANS

Boudica's troops smashed and burned as much of London as they could, then they marched up to Saint Albans to the north, and smashed and burned that too. Meanwhile, Suetonius was gathering his forces. The two armies met in the middle of England. Boudica's army left their wagons and advanced towards the Romans, but were met by a rain of Roman javelins. They were pushed back as the well-organised Roman troops approached, hemmed in by the line of wagons behind them.

FINAL DEFEAT

Boudica's brave army had finally met defeat. Thousands of British soldiers were killed. Boudica escaped the battlefield but, so the story goes, she took poison and killed herself rather than be captured by her hated Roman enemies.

SPARTACUS

Spartacus escaped from slavery and led a massive army of slave rebels that very nearly got the better of the Roman army.

HARD NUT
RATING: 8

SPARTACUS THE SLAVE

Spartacus came from Thrace (modern-day Bulgaria), but no one knows much about his early life. He became a slave and was sent to a gladiator school near Capua in Italy, where he was trained to fight in gladiatorial games for the entertainment of bloodthirsty crowds. Sometimes this meant fighting to the death, so it's no wonder Spartacus wanted to escape.

ESCAPE FROM GLADIATOR SCHOOL

Spartacus plotted an escape in 73 BC with around 200 of the other gladiators. But they were betrayed, and just as they were about to get away, the gladiator school guards leapt out to stop them. In the confusion, Spartacus and some of the others grabbed anything dangerous-looking from the kitchens they could find to use as weapons and about 70 of them managed to fight their way out.

BASHING THE ROMANS

Spartacus and two other gladiators led the desperate band of runaways to Mount Vesuvius, recruiting more slaves along the way. Roman troops arrived to meet them and camped out, waiting for the rebels to appear. Meanwhile, Spartacus and the slaves made ropes out of vines,

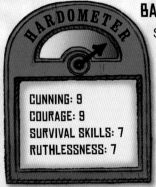

HARDOMETER

CUNNING: 9
COURAGE: 9
SURVIVAL SKILLS: 7
RUTHLESSNESS: 7

abseiled down the mountain, took the Romans by surprise from behind and defeated them. They went on to win more victories against the Romans. More and more rebellious slaves joined them until there were nearly 100,000.

THE FINAL BATTLE

The slave army split into two groups. Spartacus led one, and the other, commanded by a slave called Crixus, was completely slaughtered by the Romans – all 30,000 of them. Spartacus led his band of rebels north, fighting off Roman attacks on the way. By this time the Romans were worried: Spartacus seemed to be winning. They sent Crassus, one of their best generals, to stop him.

DEFEATED

Spartacus was finally defeated by Crassus in southern Italy in 71 BC. Six thousand rebel slaves were crucified after the battle, and thousands more were killed by Roman troops, but Spartacus' body was never found.

THERE'S NO PLACE LIKE ROME

Rome's Empire was at its biggest in AD 117, at the end of Emperor Trajan's reign and the start of Emperor Hadrian's. It stretched as far north as chilly Britain, and as far south as the sweltering deserts of North Africa – the area shaded in yellow on the map below shows this.

• The Romans first invaded Britain in 55 BC, led by Julius Caesar, but only came to stay after Emperor Claudius's invasion in AD 43.

- Rome had conquered the whole of Italy by 265 BC.

- The Romans were at war with Carthage for 100 years before finally conquering it in 146 BC.

- The Empire measured 4,000 kilometres from east to west in AD 117.

- Emperor Hadrian decided the empire was a bit too big: he set fixed frontiers to the Empire and even gave up some land in the Middle East.

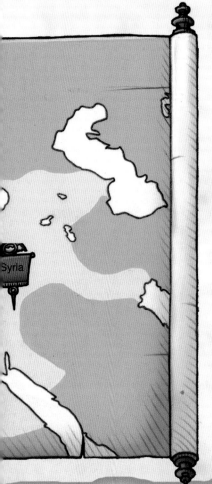

- There were plenty of hostile tribes at the edges of the Empire. Roman forts were built along the frontiers to keep marauders at bay.

- Tribes captured by the Romans were encouraged to live like the Romans but they were allowed to worship their own gods and keep their own customs. They could become Roman citizens and some of them joined the Roman army.

- The Romans often traded with barbarians (people who lived outside the Roman Empire), and came to agreements with them so they didn't fight one another.

VERCINGETORIX

Vercingetorix was a hard nut Gallic chieftain who stood up to the toughest and cleverest Roman general of them all, Julius Caesar.

HARD NUT RATING: 7.5

CONQUERING GAUL

When Julius Caesar became governor of Transalpine Gaul (in what's now southern France), the rest of Gaul wasn't under Roman control. So Caesar set about putting that right straight away. By 53 BC, he'd almost completely managed it. But that was when Vercingetorix, Gallic leader of the Arverni tribe, decided to get involved.

KING VERCINGETORIX

Vercingetorix's father had recently been executed by the Arverni for trying to make himself king. But that didn't put Vercingetorix off trying the same thing himself. He raised an army, captured the Arverni capital, Gergovia, and was proclaimed king.

CAESAR MARCHES NORTH

Vercingetorix persuaded different Gallic tribes to join forces against the Romans. Caesar marched his troops over mountains and through deep winter snow to arrive in the heart of Arverni territory. He was cold, cross and on the lookout for Vercingetorix.

HARDOMETER

CUNNING: 7
COURAGE: 8
SURVIVAL SKILLS: 7
RUTHLESSNESS: 8

RAMPAGING ROMANS AND GAULS

Caesar rampaged around the Arverni region laying waste to one town after another and killing or enslaving everyone. Vercingetorix rampaged in the opposite direction, burning all the towns behind him so that the Romans wouldn't have any food or shelter. In the spring of 52 BC, Julius Caesar besieged the Arveni capital Gergovia, but ended up losing lots of men.

GAULS VS ROMANS

The Roman forces marched south. So did Vercingetorix's army of around 100,000 – probably twice the number of Caesar's troops. But when the two sides met, the better trained and armed Romans won. Vercingetorix and his army ran away to the town of Alesia. The Romans surrounded and besieged the town, building massive great fortifications to stop anyone getting in or out. Despite his efforts to fight the Romans off, and get messages out for help, Vercingetorix was forced to surrender.

VERCINGETORIX'S END

Vercingetorix spent the next few years in prison in Rome. Caesar paraded him through the streets of Rome before finally executing him in 46 BC.

EMPEROR NERO

HARD NUT RATING: 7.8

Emperor Nero only got to be Emperor of Rome because of his mother, but he was so ruthless that he had her murdered, along with anyone else who stood in his way.

YOUNG EMPEROR

Nero became emperor when his uncle, Emperor Claudius, died in AD 54. Nero's mother, Agrippina (see page 34), had managed to get everyone else with a claim to the throne out of the way, and probably murdered Claudius, so that Nero could be emperor. At first he ruled with Agrippina because he was only sixteen. But in less than two years he'd managed to chuck her out of the imperial palace. It's also likely that Nero had his stepbrother Britannicus poisoned, because he was Emperor Claudius's son.

MORE MURDERING

To stop Agrippina from interfering, Nero took drastic measures: after a couple of failed attempts involving boats and collapsing beds, he had her assassinated. His story was that Agrippina had sent an assassin to murder him in the imperial palace because he didn't want to rule alongside her.

HARDOMETER

CUNNING: 7
COURAGE: 8
SURVIVAL SKILLS: 6
RUTHLESSNESS: 10

PARTY TIME

With his mother out of the way, Nero concentrated on what he was good at: chariot

racing, music, poetry, and partying. He divorced his wife,
Octavia, had her executed, married his girlfriend Poppaea,
and embarked on expensive building programmes and
entertainment, which swallowed large amounts of money
raised by taxes. People started to get annoyed with Nero.

THE GREAT FIRE OF ROME

In AD 64, fire spread through Rome. Nero didn't seem too
bothered and so he became even less popular. Unwisely, he
started a grand building programme on the site of the fire,
which included the Golden House, a luxurious new palace
for himself. To pay for it, he took treasure from temples
around the empire, which caused a rebellion in Jerusalem.

THE LAST STRAW

While Nero was on a tour of Greece, everyone decided they
had had enough. The Senate condemned him to be flogged
to death in AD 69. Rather than face his grisly sentence,
Nero fled. It's thought that he took his own life by cutting
his throat.

SCIPIO THE GREAT

Scipio was a fearsome Roman general who finally defeated the Carthaginian hard nut Hannibal, and ended the Second Punic War.

HARD NUT
RATING: 8.8

ROMAN DEFEATS

Scipio came from a long line of warlike Scipios – his grandfather and father did their fair share of fighting in the war with Carthage, the tough North African empire that Rome was determined to conquer. At the Battle of Ticinus, 18-year-old Scipio saved his father's life. But things were not going well for the Romans: they lost the battle, and went on to even worse defeats at the hands of Carthaginian general Hannibal (see page 8). In 211 BC, Scipio's father and uncle were both killed in battle with the Carthaginians in Spain.

SCIPIO IN SPAIN

No one else in Rome much fancied leading the Roman army in Spain against the ferocious Carthaginians. But Scipio was tough enough to take the job. Once he was given command of his own troops, he never lost a battle.

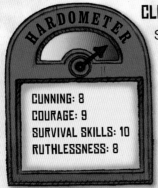

HARDOMETER

CUNNING: 8
COURAGE: 9
SURVIVAL SKILLS: 10
RUTHLESSNESS: 8

CLOBBERING THE CARTHAGINIANS

Scipio battered the Carthaginians at Ilipa in the south of Spain in 206 BC. By the end of the year, his army had managed to push the Carthaginians out of Spain completely. In 205 BC he was made consul, and persuaded Rome that he should invade North Africa while Hannibal was busy rampaging around Italy causing as much damage as he could.

AFRICAN VICTORY

Hannibal returned from Italy in 202 BC to fight Scipio near Carthage at the Battle of Zama. Despite Hannibal's eighty war elephants, Scipio won. He conquered the northern part of Africa, and ended the Second Punic War with Carthage. He returned to Rome in triumph, and was given an extra name, after his conquest: Scipio Africanus.

RETIRING FROM ROME

Scipio and his brother, Scipio Asiaticus, led another Roman victory, this time in Syria. Despite his victories, though, Scipio didn't stay in favour in Rome, and went to live in the south of Italy. He died about 183 BC, probably in the same year as his old enemy, Hannibal.

SCIPIO AFRICANUS

THE RISE AND FALL OF THE ROMAN EMPIRE

It took hundreds of years for the city of Rome to grow into a whacking great empire, and another few hundred years for it to get battered by barbarians.

ROMULUS AND REMUS

About 3,000 years ago, people settled on the hilltops above the River Tiber in Italy. Their villages gradually grew into the city of Rome. But in Roman legend, two twins, Romulus and Remus, were abandoned by their parents but saved and brought up by a female wolf; after a terrible fight, Romulus killed Remus and went on to found the city of Rome, named after himself.

KICKING OUT THE KINGS

Rome was ruled by kings, until the Roman people got fed up with them and kicked them out. The last king was Tarquin the Proud, whose reign ended in 509 BC. Rome became a republic, ruled by elected politicians headed by two Consuls.

A BIT OF CONQUERING

By about 265 BC the Romans had conquered the rest of Italy and started on other countries. Some of them put up quite a fight but eventually Rome controlled most of the land around the Mediterranean Sea.

GENERALS AND EMPERORS

After 500 years as a republic, things began to change in Rome. Julius Caesar became almost like a king, until he was stabbed to death. It wasn't long before the end of the Roman Republic and the start of the Roman Empire. The first Emperor was Augustus Caesar, Julius Caesar's adopted son.

AN ENORMOUS EMPIRE

There was already quite a big empire waiting for the first Roman Emperor. After more conquering the Empire kept growing until, in the reign of the fourteenth Emperor, Hadrian, it reached the biggest it would ever be.

I HATE BATH TIME.

EAST AND WEST

At the end of the 200s the Empire was split into an eastern and a western empire, both of which were attacked by barbarian tribes. In 476 the last emperor of the Western Roman Empire was chucked out by the barbarian, Odoacer. But the Eastern Roman Empire (also known as the Byzantine Empire) lasted until the middle of the fifteenth century.

SULLA

Sulla was one of Rome's toughest and most ruthless leaders. He was most famous for his brutal executions.

HARD NUT RATING: 10

NOBBLING NUMIDIANS

Sulla's first big victory was against hard nut King Jugurtha of Numidia, in North Africa, who had successfully battered the Roman army in 111 and 110 BC. Sulla ended the conflict by persuading another African king to betray and kidnap Jugurtha for the Romans. But Marius, who was commanding the campaign, got the credit for the Roman victory. This started a rivalry between Sulla and Marius that was to be a major clash of the hard nuts.

MARCHING ON ROME

Sulla gained a reputation as a toughie, and in 87 BC he was sent off to sort out King Mithradites of Pontus, who was causing problems for Rome in the area that's now north-western Turkey. Marius was cross: *he* had wanted the chance to batter King Mithradites and get the glory. So he persuaded the Senate to call Sulla back. Sulla was absolutely furious. So furious that he marched on Rome at the head of six legions. This meant civil war! He lost no time in taking control of the city. Then Sulla dusted himself down and went back to Pontus to finish his business with King Mithradites.

HARDOMETER

CUNNING: 10
COURAGE: 10
SURVIVAL SKILLS: 10
RUTHLESSNESS: 10

DICTATOR OF ROME

Meanwhile, with Sulla away, Marius led his own march on Rome to try and capture the city himself. He caused a lot of death and destruction, and outlawed Sulla, but he died the following year. Sulla, even more cross by this time, marched on Rome again. Helped by the generals Crassus and Pompey (see page 43) he ended the civil war once and for all. Sulla was now dictator of Rome.

SULLA'S EXECUTIONS

Sulla began a reign of terror. He drew up lists of his enemies – proscriptions – including anyone he thought couldn't be counted on to support him. Then he had them executed. He was accused of proscribing rich people just so that he could nick their possessions. In the end, thousands were killed in Sulla's proscriptions. Perhaps worn out with all that executing, Sulla stepped down from office in 79 BC, and died the following year.

PROSCRIPTIONS

FLAVIUS AETIUS

Flavius Aetius was a barbarian-bashing general who led the Roman army in the last desperate years of the Western Roman Empire.

HARD NUT
RATING: 8.5

MARAUDING BARBARIANS

By the AD 400s, the Roman Empire had divided into two. Things were not going well, especially in the Western Empire, and barbarian tribes made constant attacks. When they weren't fighting the marauding barbarians, the Romans were making pacts with them to keep them quiet. From AD 405-408, when Flavius Aetius was a teenager, he was sent as a hostage to Alaric I, King of the Visigoths. Noble Roman hostages such as Aetius were like a promise that the Romans would keep to their side of the agreement. Then, in a similar arrangement, Aetius went to stay with the Huns – and ended up living and fighting alongside them for years.

VALENTINIAN, VISIGOTHS AND FRANKS

Aetius was made commander of the Roman army in Gaul, which was just the sort of job he liked, since it gave him the perfect opportunity to batter barbarians. First he drove back the Visigoths, then he defeated the Franks . . . then the Visigoths again, and then the Franks again. Meanwhile, Aetius was worried that another hard nut general, Bonifacius, might be doing better than he was – so he marched against him and defeated him. Aetius was now the most powerful

HARDOMETER

CUNNING: 9
COURAGE: 9
SURVIVAL SKILLS: 7
RUTHLESSNESS: 9

general and politician in the Western Roman Empire, though Valentinian III, a young boy whose mother ruled as regent, was the Emperor.

ATTILA ATTACKS

The next few years saw plenty more barbarian bashing. Attila was leader of Aetius' old friends the Huns. He was on good terms with Aetius, but eventually Attila couldn't resist it any longer: he attacked Gaul. Aetius persuaded the Visigoths to join him against the Huns, and in AD 451 the Romans and Visigoths defeated them. The following year Attila was back, rampaging around Italy, until eventually he was chased away by Aetius' army.

VALENTINIAN GETS VIOLENT

Aetius didn't die in battle. Valentinian grew up to be suspicious of him: he thought Aetius wanted his own son to be emperor. In AD 454 he leapt at him with a sword, accusing him of treason, and killed him. Six months later, Valentinian was killed by a Hun assassin.

AGRIPPINA

Agrippina rose to be the most
powerful woman in Rome,
and she got there by plotting,
scheming, and probably poisoning.

**HARD NUT
RATING: 8.8**

THE EMPEROR'S SISTER

Agrippina the Younger was the great-granddaughter of the
first Roman Emperor, Augustus Caesar. When she was 21,
her brother Caligula became emperor. He gave Agrippina
and her two sisters, Drusilla and Livilla, special privileges,
but when Drusilla died of a sudden illness Caligula stopped
being so nice to the other two. Instead, he started
behaving very strangely: he demanded to be worshipped
as a god, made his horse a priest, and ordered his army to
collect seashells.

PLOT OF THE THREE DAGGERS

Agrippina didn't like the way things were turning out. She,
her sister and their cousin Lepidus plotted to murder
Caligula and make Lepidus emperor. But the 'Plot of the
Three Daggers' was discovered. Lepidus was executed and
the two sisters were exiled.

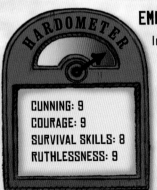

HARDOMETER

CUNNING: 9
COURAGE: 9
SURVIVAL SKILLS: 8
RUTHLESSNESS: 9

EMPEROR UNCLE CLAUDIUS

In AD 41, Caligula was murdered
by his own bodyguard. Claudius,
Agrippina's uncle, became
emperor, and called the sisters
back to Rome. Agrippina married
a rich and powerful man, who
died a few years later. The
rumour was that she'd poisoned
her husband to get his money.

EMPRESS OF ROME

Emperor Claudius's wife Messalina was executed in AD 48 for plotting to kill him. Even though she was his niece, Agrippina married Claudius the next year, to become the most powerful woman in Rome – the Empress. She persuaded Claudius to adopt her son by her first marriage, Nero, as his heir instead of his own three children.

MORE MURDERING

The story goes that Agrippina poisoned Claudius with toxic mushrooms when he began to regret marrying her. This meant her son Nero became emperor of Rome. But he didn't thank his mother for putting him there, and threw Agrippina out of the imperial palace as quickly as he could.

YOU LIKE MUSHROOMS, DON'T YOU DARLING?

EVEN MORE MURDERING

There's a story that Agrippina swam to shore after Nero sank a boat she was travelling on, and that she survived another murder attempt by her son when he rigged a bed to collapse on top of her. Finally, Nero sent assassins to kill her, and Agrippina died in AD 59.

THE GOOD GOD GUIDE

The Romans worshipped lots of gods and goddesses – about 20 main ones, mostly borrowed from the ancient Greeks, but given Roman names. For example, Zeus, the Greek king of the gods, was the Roman god Jupiter; the Greek goddess of love, Aphrodite, was the Roman goddess Venus; Ares, the Greek god of war, was the Roman god of Mars.

LOTS OF GODS

There were also household gods who protected the home, gods of the food cupboard, and even a god of a type of mould that attacks wheat (there was an annual festival to please him so that the corn would be spared). Abstract qualities, like Discipline and Youth were worshipped as gods too. Some Emperors had themselves made into gods after they'd died, including Augustus, Trajan, Hadrian and Claudius.

TRUE OR FALSE?

How many of these goddesses do you think are real, and how many made up?

- Cloacina, goddess of sewers
- Annona, goddess of the grain supply to the city of Rome
- Cardea, goddess of door hinges
- Bubona, goddess of cattle
- Iris, goddess of the rainbow
- Mellona, goddess of bees
- Nemesis, goddess of revenge
- Devera, goddess of brooms used to purify temples

FOUL FESTIVALS

In honour of all those gods, the Romans had lots of festivals. They often included animal sacrifices to please the gods. A haruspex was a Roman priest who made predictions about the future by looking at the splattered innards of sacrificed animals.

EVEN MORE GODS

The Romans were happy to add foreign gods of countries they'd conquered to their huge collection. At least this meant one less thing to argue about with the natives. Near Hadrian's Wall, for example, the Romans set up a shrine to Brigantia, goddess of a northern British tribe. Mithraism was a Persian religion that became popular with the Roman army. Eventually, with Constantine the Great, the Romans adopted Christianity as their main religion.

Answers: They're all real Roman goddesses.

MARK ANTONY

HARD NUT
RATING: 8

A tough Roman army commander and persuasive politician, Mark Antony became one of the most powerful men in the world, before losing everything to Augustus Caesar.

CONQUERING GAUL AND GOVERNING ITALY

Mark Antony charged into hard nut history leading cavalry in Judea and Egypt, and later fought alongside his distant relative, Julius Caesar (see page 12), in his conquest of Gaul. He governed Italy while Caesar was off conquering, and he fought with Caesar in his victory over Pompey (see page 43) at the Battle of Pharsalus.

OVER CAESAR'S DEAD BODY

Caesar tried to make himself dictator for life, which upset some senators so much that they stabbed him to death in 44 BC. Mark Antony gave a rousing speech at his funeral, pointing out Caesar's stab wounds and naming the senators who had made each one.

THREE'S A CROWD

HARDOMETER

CUNNING: 8
COURAGE: 9
SURVIVAL SKILLS: 7
RUTHLESSNESS: 8

Mark Antony formed a three-man alliance (a 'triumvirate') with Marcus Aemilius Lepidus and Caesar's heir, Octavian, and took control of Rome. When the Senate tried to kick them out, they had 130 senators murdered. The triumvirate also had to deal with two of Caesar's old enemies, Cassius and Brutus, and defeated them in battle in 42 BC.

Octavian returned to Rome, Antony looked after Roman territory in the east, and Lepidus took control of Spain and North Africa.

TROUBLESOME WOMEN

When Mark Antony's wife Fulvia had an argument with Octavian, she didn't just shout and storm off: she raised eight legions and fought a battle against him. Octavian won, though, and Mark Antony divorced Fulvia and married Octavia, Octavian's sister. But then he upset them both – he went to Egypt and fell in love with Cleopatra.

BATTLE OF ACTIUM

Octavian fell out with Mark Antony, and forced Lepidus to resign. Cleopatra claimed that hers and Julius Caesar's son, Caesarion, was the true heir to the Roman Empire, and Mark Antony supported her, so they went to war with Octavian. At the Battle of Actium, Octavian won and Mark Antony killed himself. Rather than be brought as a prisoner to Rome, Cleopatra killed herself too.

TARQUIN THE PROUD

Tarquin was a ruthless, murderous, greedy tyrant. No wonder he was the last king of Rome.

HARD NUT
RATING: 8.3

LEGENDARY KINGS

According to Roman tradition, the first King of Rome was Romulus, who'd been reared by a she-wolf before he founded Rome. Some of what we know about Tarquin the Proud might be legendary, too. He was the seventh King of Rome, who ruled from 534 to 509 BC.

MURDER IN THE FAMILY

Tarquin was either the son or grandson of the fifth King of Rome, but he was passed over in favour of Servius Tullius. Servius Tullius gave his two daughters to be married to Tarquin and his brother, but Tarquin and his brother's wife, Tullia, decided they preferred one another: they had Tarquin's brother and Tullia's sister murdered, then married one another. Then Tarquin had Servius Tullius murdered so that he could take his place as king. The story goes that Tullia ran over Servius Tullius' body – her own father – with her chariot.

HARDOMETER

CUNNING: 8
COURAGE: 7
SURVIVAL SKILLS: 9
RUTHLESSNESS: 9

TERRIBLE TIMES

Tarquin began his reign by murdering any senators he suspected of supporting the previous king. This reduced the size of the Senate, and he ruled as a dictator. He conquered towns surrounding Rome and took their wealth, which the

Romans probably wouldn't have minded, but they did mind that he hadn't asked them first. Eventually, a group of senators rebelled against Tarquin and kicked him out in 509 BC.

REPUBLICAN ROME

The Roman Republic, with elected leaders called consuls, began. Tarquin sent his sons to start a conspiracy, but that didn't work and the sons were executed. Next Tarquin stirred up trouble with Rome's neighbouring cities, and led attacks on Rome. He was defeated at the Battle of Silva Arsia, but he didn't give up. He persuaded Lars Porsenna of Clusium to attack Rome – and this time the Romans were beaten. They still wouldn't have Tarquin back, though.

FINAL DEFEAT

Tarquin turned to his son-in-law, who ruled a group of Latin villages near Rome, for help. When Rome beat the Latins, Tarquin finally admitted defeat. He skulked off to stay with the Greek tyrant, Aristodemus of Cumae, where he died the following year, in 495 BC.

POMPEY THE GREAT

Pompey was a great general and politician, but finally met his downfall against Julius Caesar.

HARD NUT RATING: 8.8

TAKING SIDES

Pompey was born in Rome in 106 BC, and lost no time in showing he was a rough, tough conquering Roman. He sided with ruthless general Sulla (see page 30) in Sulla's civil war against Marius, and led victories for him in Africa and Sicily. He ruthlessly executed Marius's generals if they surrendered, and earned the nickname 'Sulla's butcher' from his enemies.

TRIUMPH, CONQUERING AND CRUSHING

Pompey was given a 'triumph' – a parade through the city of Rome to celebrate his victory, which gave him a chance to show off. When Sulla stepped down from being dictator of Rome, Pompey went to Spain to fight against one of Marius's generals, and re-conquered Spain. By now he was very powerful. He came back to Italy in time to help crush Spartacus's rebellion (see page 18), and was made consul in 70 BC, together with his rival Crassus.

HARDOMETER

CUNNING: 9
COURAGE: 9
SURVIVAL SKILLS: 8
RUTHLESSNESS: 9

POMPEY'S PIRATES

Pirates were a menace in the Mediterranean Sea, and Pompey was the obvious choice to solve the problem. Having taken control of the Mediterranean for Rome with a minimum of fuss, and helped resettle the pirates so that they wouldn't come back, Pompey was off to fight King Mithradates in Pontus. He also made an alliance with the Armenians, captured Jerusalem, and made Syria a Roman province. Phew.

POMPEY, CRASSUS AND CAESAR

In 59 BC Pompey joined Crassus and Caesar to form a three-man alliance and married Julia, Julius Caesar's daughter. But by 54 BC, Julia had died, and Crassus was killed in battle. Pompey and Julius Caesar competed for power. Pompey persuaded the senators to back him instead of Caesar. The senate asked Caesar to give up his army. In reply, Caesar marched his army on Rome, declaring himself at war with Pompey.

LOSING HIS HEAD

Pompey met Julius Caesar at the Battle of Pharsalus. Although Caesar had a smaller army and his soldiers were tired, he managed to outwit Pompey, and won. Pompey was forced to run away to Egypt. But the Egyptian leader Ptolemy betrayed him: he killed Pompey, cut off his head and offered it to Caesar as a gift.

I HAVE A LOT TO DO SO JUST BEHAVE YOURSELF!

THE ROMAN EMPIRE GAME

For two to six players. You'll need a counter each and a dice to play this game.

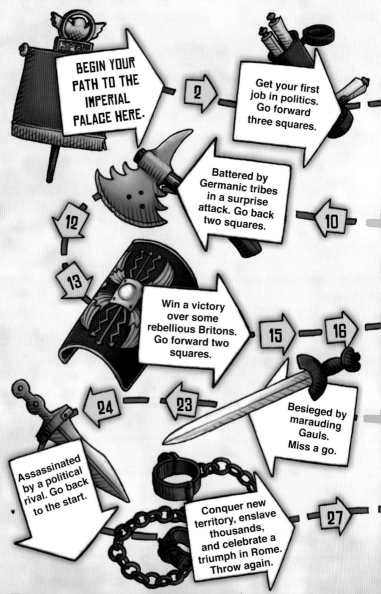

BEGIN YOUR PATH TO THE IMPERIAL PALACE HERE.

2

Get your first job in politics. Go forward three squares.

Battered by Germanic tribes in a surprise attack. Go back two squares.

12

10

13

Win a victory over some rebellious Britons. Go forward two squares.

15

16

24

23

Besieged by marauding Gauls. Miss a go.

Assassinated by a political rival. Go back to the start.

Conquer new territory, enslave thousands, and celebrate a triumph in Rome. Throw again.

27

You're ambitious Roman citizens on the path to power in the Roman Empire. Which of you will be hard enough to fight, persuade, conquer and murder your way to the top?

4

Pirates attack in the Mediterranean Sea. Go back three squares.

6

Given command of the army in Gaul. Go forward three squares.

EXILE

9

Forced into exile when your political opponent gets into power. Miss a go.

18

Struck down by plague. Miss two goes.

Elected consul. Throw again.

21

Marry the Emperor's daughter. Go forward four squares.

Murder your main rival. Go forward two squares.

29

The Emperor dies and the army wants YOU to take his place. HAIL CAESAR!

CARACTACUS

British chieftain Caractacus was not happy about the Roman invasion and so did something about it in the only way he knew how.

HARD NUT
RATING: 8.8

THE ROMANS ARRIVE

Caractacus was chieftain of the Catuvellauni tribe in southeast England. The Romans invaded in AD 43 under Emperor Claudius, and made agreements with British leaders who were happy to accept Roman rule.

FRIENDLY ROMANS

To many of the British chieftains, Roman rule seemed like a fair deal – they got the protection of the Roman army and could keep their own religion and customs. Plus, the Romans wouldn't kill them. But Caractacus didn't agree with Roman rule. He began to attack Roman-friendly tribes, including King Verica of the Atrebates tribe.

ROMANS VS BRITONS

King Verica fled to Rome and asked Emperor Claudius to help fight Caractacus. Claudius arrived in Britain with a force of 40,000 soldiers. They landed in Kent, where they faced an army of Britons including Caractacus. The Romans won and most of the defeated tribes came to agreements with Claudius, and accepted the Romans.

HARDOMETER

CUNNING: 8
COURAGE: 9
SURVIVAL SKILLS: 10
RUTHLESSNESS: 8

CARACTACUS GOES WEST

But not Caractacus. He went westwards until he found another tribe that was hard enough to join him – the Silures, from modern-day South Wales. The Romans had a better equipped and better trained army, but Caractacus had the advantage of knowing the country. In AD 50 he gathered together an army of his own tribe, the Silures, and anyone else he could persuade to stand up to the Romans.

WELSH DEFEAT

Caractacus gave a rousing speech, reminding his troops that their ancestors had already driven out one lot of Romans, Julius Caesar's, over a hundred years before. The British forces met the Romans bravely and fiercely, but the Roman army was just too good for them. Caractacus tried to find refuge with Cartimandua, Queen of the Brigantes, but he was caught, put in chains and handed over to the Romans.

HAPPY ENDING

Amazingly, rather than execute Caractacus, Claudius spared him and his family, who had a happy retirement in southern Italy.

EMPEROR TRAJAN

Thanks to Trajan's relentless conquering, the Roman Empire grew to be the biggest it would ever be.

HARD NUT RATING: 8.5

TRAJAN'S HERO

Trajan became emperor in AD 98. His hero was Julius Caesar (see page 12), famous for winning new territory for Rome. Trajan lost no time in doing some conquering of his own.

EMPIRE BUILDING

Trajan was an experienced soldier. He was 45 by the time he became emperor, and he'd already commanded the Roman army in northwestern Spain, and sorted out a rebellion by the Roman governor of Germany. He started by making Arabia Petraea under Roman control (the area that's now the Sinai peninsula, plus bits of Jordan and Saudia Arabia). Then he led his army against King Decebalus of Dacia (modern-day Romania), and successfully conquered the country, which happened to contain several gold mines. To celebrate, King Decebalus's head was put on display in Rome, and Trajan's column was built – a thirty-metre-tall column sculpted with glorious highlights from the war with Dacia.

HARDOMETER

CUNNING: 8
COURAGE: 9
SURVIVAL SKILLS: 9
RUTHLESSNESS: 8

MORE CONQUERING

But Trajan wasn't finished yet and went on to conquer Mesopotamia (modern-day Iraq) as well. Trajan also fought

Mesopotamia's neighbour, Parthia (modern-day Iran), and conquered bits of that too.

LOOT!

All that conquering meant that Rome collected treasure and slaves – half a million of them. With the loot from the conquered lands, Trajan introduced help for poor children, reduced the amount people had to pay in tax, and built new and impressive buildings in Rome. He also introduced a gruesome three-month-long festival in the Colosseum in Rome, in which chariot racing and fights with gladiators and wild animals provided blood-thirsty entertainment.

NO MORE CONQUERING

Trajan had done more conquering than any other Roman. But finally, just before he had a chance to finish off the Parthians for good, he died suddenly in AD 117. The Roman Empire was now at its biggest, and the Roman army consisted of 400,000 men.

GALEN

Galen is the only ancient Roman hard nut who didn't kill people – at least, not on purpose. He was the most famous ancient Roman doctor ever.

HARD NUT RATING: 7.5

WOUNDED GLADIATORS

As a young man, Galen studied medicine in Greece and Alexandria in Egypt before returning to Pergamum (in modern-day Turkey) where he was born. He became chief doctor at the local gladiator school, so he had plenty of wounds to practise on. He called the gladiators' wounds 'windows into the body' and healed them so successfully that only five gladiators died in the five years he was their doctor.

DOCTORS AND PATIENTS

In around AD 162, Galen moved to Rome. The other Roman doctors didn't like his new-fangled ideas and plotted against him. Galen was so worried that they might poison him that he left Rome. But Emperor Marcus Aurelius called him back to become the doctor of the imperial court, and he remained the Emperor's doctor and for the two Emperors who followed too.

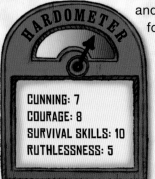

HARDOMETER

CUNNING: 7
COURAGE: 8
SURVIVAL SKILLS: 10
RUTHLESSNESS: 5

KIDNEYS, LUNGS AND CATARACTS

When he wasn't treating emperors, Galen experimented: he dissected animals, used bellows to inflate dead animals' lungs, and was especially interested in the spinal cords of pigs. He discovered that urine is formed inside kidneys (people thought it was formed in the bladder), and found out what larynxes are for (so that we can speak), and that arteries carry blood. He was also a skilled surgeon, and performed delicate operations to remove cataracts from patients' eyes.

THE PLAGUE OF GALEN

One of the reasons Marcus Aurelius called Galen to Rome was an outbreak of plague, which swept through the Roman Empire. There were millions of deaths from the plague, with up to 2,000 people dying a day in Rome. Galen lived through the outbreak, treated its victims and recorded its deadly progress. Today the disease is thought to have been smallpox.

LASTING LEGACY

Galen lived until he was quite old – at least 70. His medical theories were still being used 1,500 years after his death.

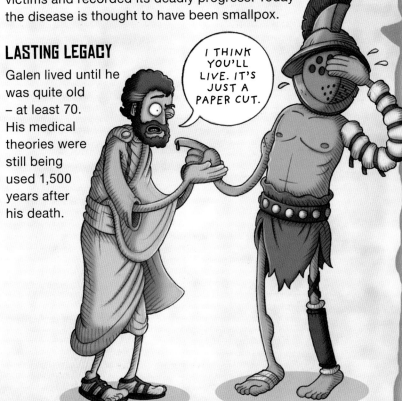

I THINK YOU'LL LIVE. IT'S JUST A PAPER CUT.

ZENOBIA

Zenobia was a warrior queen. She revolted against the Romans, conquered Egypt, and built up her own empire.

HARD NUT
RATING: 8.8

QUEEN ZENOBIA

Around AD 258, Zenobia married the King of Palmyra in Syria. Nine years later, the king and his son from a previous marriage were both assassinated, so Queen Zenobia ruled instead, with her one-year-old son, Vaballathus. Palmyra's neighbour was the Sassanid Empire, which was based in what's now Iran, but was rapidly expanding, and causing trouble for the Romans in the process. Zenobia fought the Sassanids, saying that she was protecting the Eastern Roman Empire – though really she was winning new land for her own empire.

CONQUERING!

In AD 269 Zenobia rode into battle with her army and conquered Egypt, with the help of an Egyptian friend, Timagenes, and his army. She proclaimed herself Queen of Egypt, and became known for her bravery, horse-riding skills and as a warrior queen. But she didn't stop there: next Zenobia and the Palmyrenes conquered a big chunk of Anatolia (in modern-day Turkey), then Syria, Palestine and Lebanon in the Middle East.

HARDOMETER

CUNNING: 9
COURAGE: 9
SURVIVAL SKILLS: 9
RUTHLESSNESS: 8

ZENOBIA VS THE ROMANS

The Romans, under Emperor Aurelian, had enough trouble from the Sassanids and their expanding Empire, and were absolutely furious to discover that Zenobia had started conquering her own empire as well. They came to meet her near Antioch (a city that's now in Turkey), and defeated the Palmyrene army.

ESCAPE AND CAPTURE

Zenobia escaped by camel, but was soon captured by the Roman cavalry. Her Palmyrene Empire had been defeated before it had had a chance to get going. Any Palmyrenes who didn't surrender to the Romans were executed, and Zenobia and her son Vabathallus were taken to Rome. In AD 274 Zenobia appeared in golden chains in Rome, so that everyone could see Emperor Aurelian's conquest.

ZENOBIA'S END

No one is sure of what happened to Zenobia. There's a story that Aurelian was so impressed by Zenobia's bravery and beauty that he gave her a villa in Italy, where she married and lived a happy life. But no one knows for sure.

FLAVIUS BELISARIUS

HARD NUT RATING: 9

Flavius Belisarius was the greatest general of the Eastern Roman Empire, who re-conquered huge chunks of the old Roman Empire.

EASTERN COMMANDER

By the time Belisarius was born, the Western Roman Empire had already fallen to barbarians, and the Eastern Roman Empire, or Byzantine Empire, was ruled from Constantinople (modern-day Istanbul in Turkey). Belisarius joined the army under the Eastern Roman Emperor Justin I, and did so well that the next emperor, Justinian I, gave him command of the whole army.

REBELLIONS, PERSIANS AND VANDALS

In AD 532, when Belisarius was 27, there was an uprising in Constantinople and Belisarius was sent to stop it. By the time Belisarius had dealt with it, around 30,000 people had been killed. He went on to win a series of brilliant victories against the Persians. Then Belisarius lost no time in driving the Vandals out of Africa, making the African provinces (Eastern) Roman once again.

HARDOMETER

CUNNING: 9
COURAGE: 9
SURVIVAL SKILLS: 9
RUTHLESSNESS: 9

OSTROGOTHS IN ITALY

It was a busy few years for Belisarius, because in AD 535 he was sent to fight the Ostrogoths in Italy. Once he'd defeated them, the Ostrogoths wanted to make him their king. Belisarius pretended to go along with the idea, then had the Ostrogoth leaders arrested and claimed their empire for Emperor Justinian.

JEALOUS JUSTINIAN

Belisarius fought the Persians again, then he was back to Italy to crush a Goth rebellion in Rome. Belisarius captured the city, but Emperor Justinian called him back to Constantinople – he was worried that the handsome, charming general was too popular. Even after Belisarius had fought back the invading Bulgars in AD 559, Emperor Justinian wasn't happy. He accused Belisarius of made-up charges, and sent him to prison.

TOUGHEST EASTERN NUT

After all that conquering, rebellion-crushing and invader-repelling, Belisarius was pardoned. He died three years later in AD 565, at the age of 60, having won the admiration of just about everyone as the toughest nut of the Eastern Roman Empire.

ARE YOU KIDDING ME?

EMPEROR HADRIAN

Hadrian inherited a vast empire. He fortified its frontiers, and made sure his army was hard enough to hang on to it.

HARD NUT RATING: 8.5

EXPANDED EMPIRE

Hadrian had commanded troops in empire-expanding Trajan's battles and Trajan had made him governor of Syria. He became emperor of Rome when Trajan died, and the first thing he did was to have several senators killed, accusing them of conspiring against him. Because of Trajan's conquering, the empire had grown so big that Hadrian decided it needed to shrink a bit, and gave up Rome's new eastern territories in Mesopotamia.

TOUGH TROOPS

Hadrian was very keen on keeping a tough, fit, well-trained and well-disciplined army, and spent as much time with the soldiers as he could, showing them that he could be just as tough as them. Hadrian travelled around his empire with his army, but rather than conquering he concentrated on making its borders secure from marauders.

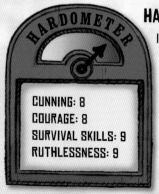

CUNNING: 8
COURAGE: 8
SURVIVAL SKILLS: 9
RUTHLESSNESS: 9

HADRIAN'S WALL

In AD 122, Hadrian decided to take a trip somewhere cold, damp and a stone's throw from marauding hostile tribes: Britain. He looked at the borderline of his empire, a road called the Stanegate that stretched across the north of Britain, then he looked at what was on the other side: a bleak landscape full of angry-looking natives. So he ordered a huge stone wall to be built – one that would keep the barbarians where they belonged – Hadrian's Wall.

WAR ON JERUSALEM

Hadrian waged one war while he was emperor, and he did it with utter ruthlessness. In AD 130, he visited the ruins of Jerusalem (there had been a Roman-Jewish war that ended in 73) and rebuilt the city. But his anti-Jewish laws sparked a revolt, and a fierce war raged for three years. After the war Hadrian sold many thousands of captured Jews into slavery, and continued to make anti-Jewish laws. Three years later, in AD 138, Hadrian died, leaving his slightly reduced empire to his heir, Antoninus Pius.

HARD NUTS OF ANCIENT ROME TIMELINE

753 BC

According to legend, the year Rome was founded by Romulus. It was ruled by kings until . . .

509 BC

. . .Tarquin the Proud, the last King of Rome, was kicked off the throne.

264 BC

The first Punic War began, fought between Carthage and Rome. The Punic Wars continued until 146 BC.

247 BC

Hannibal, the Carthaginian general, was born.

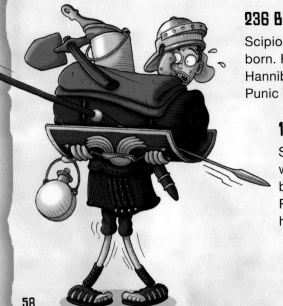

236 BC

Scipio the Great was born. He defeated Hannibal in the Second Punic War.

138 BC

Sulla was born. He was a general who became dictator of Rome and executed his enemies.

109 BC

The leader of the slave rebellion of 73 BC, Spartacus, was born.

106 BC

Pompey, the Roman general and leader, was born.

100 BC

Julius Caesar was born. He was assassinated by a group of senators in 44 BC.

83 BC

Mark Antony was born. He killed himself after the Battle of Actium.

82 BC

Vercingetorix, the Gaulish chieftain who fought Julius Caesar, was born.

63 BC

Augustus Caesar was born.

32 BC

The Battle of Actium between Octavian and Cleopatra – afterwards Octavian became Augustus, the 'First Citizen' (really the first Emperor) of Rome.

AD 10

Around this date, British leader Caractacus was born.

AD 15 OR 16

Agrippina, mother of Emperor Nero, was born.

AD 30

British warrior queen, Boudica, was born around this date.

AD 37

Emperor Nero was born.

AD 43

The Romans invade Britain under Emperor Claudius.

AD 53

Emperor Trajan was born. He made the Roman Empire the biggest it would ever be.

AD 76

Emperor Hadrian was born.

AD 130

Galen, the famous Roman doctor, was born.

AD 240

Zenobia, warrior queen of Palmyra, was born.

AD 285

The Emperor Diocletian divided the Roman Empire in two: the Western Roman Empire and the Eastern Roman Empire.

AD 396

Roman general Flavius Aetius was born.

AD 476

The last emperor of the Western Roman Empire was thrown out by barbarian leader Odoacer. The Eastern Roman Empire continued until 1453, when it was overthrown by the Ottoman Empire.

AD 505

Eastern Roman general, Flavius Belisarius, was born.

GLOSSARY

ASSASSINS People who commit murder in a surprise attack (usually for political reasons)

BARBARIANS Tribesmen who are seen by others as being uncivilized and primitive

BESIEGED Surrounded by enemy forces

CENTURION A soldier who is in charge of a century (a group of 80 legionaries) in the Roman army

COHORTS Groups of soldiers in the Roman army. Six centuries (groups of 80 legionaries) make up a consort

CONSUL The highest ruler of ancient Rome

CRUCIFIED Killed by being nailed or tied to a cross and left to die

ELECTED Chosen to be leader

EMPIRE A group of states or countries ruled by one leader or state

GLADIATOR An armed person who fought with others (often to the death) in public, to entertain the audience

HOSTAGES People who are captured and held by someone who demands that certain things are done before they are freed

LEGION A group of 5120 soldiers in the Roman army, consisting of nine cohorts and one prima cohors

LEGIONARY A foot soldier in the Roman army

MARAUDING Going about in search of things to steal or people to attack

OUTLAWED Banned

PARDONED Forgiven or excused

PRIMA COHORS A group of soldiers in the Roman army. Ten centuries (groups of 80 legionaries) make up a prima cohors

PROSCRIBE Ban or condemn

REPUBLIC A country ruled without a king or queen

REVOLT A rebellion

SENATE A group of 300 people (senators) acting as advisors to the consuls (leaders) of Rome (the consuls were chosen from the Senate)

SENATOR One of 300 members of the Senate

TREASON Betraying one's country by going to war against it or helping its enemies

TRIUMVIRATE A group of three men holding power

INDEX